CLUE BOOKS

Flowers

Gwen Allen   Joan Denslow

OXFORD UNIVERSITY PRESS

Oxford University Press, Great Clarendon Street, Oxford OX2 6DP

Oxford New York
Athens Auckland Bangkok Bogotá Bombay
Buenos Aires Calcutta Cape Town Dar es Salaam
Delhi Florence Hong Kong Istanbul Karachi
Kuala Lumpur Madras Madrid Melbourne
Mexico City Nairobi Paris Singapore
Taipei Tokyo Toronto

and associated companies in
Berlin Ibadan

Oxford is a trade mark of Oxford University Press

© Oxford University Press 1997
First published 1970
New edition 1997

CLUE BOOKS – FLOWERS
produced for Oxford University Press
by Bender Richardson White, Uxbridge

Editors: Lionel Bender, John Stidworthy Design: Ben White
Media Conversion and Page Make-up: MW Graphics
Project Manager: Kim Richardson
Original artwork: Rosemary Lee and Tim Halliday
Additional artwork: Ron Hayward, Clive Pritchard

A CIP catalogue record for this book is available from the British Library

ISBN 0-19-910175-2 (hardback)   ISBN 0-19-910181-7 (paperback)

1 3 5 7 9 10 8 6 4 2

Printed in Italy

CONTENTS

ABOUT THIS BOOK

This book is about wild flowering plants that are common in northern and western Europe. It allows you to identify the plants by their flowers and it tells you what time of the year and where you may see the plants. In order to use this book you will need to look at real flowers and their component parts. A magnifying lens will help you to see flower parts more clearly.

The book is divided into an Introduction and seven sections, each looking at groups of plants with similar flower structures. Within each section are two parts: Clues and Identification. The Introduction describes and illustrates flower structure and the basic arrangements on plants of fruits and leaves. Each set of Clues, starting on page 8, allows you to identify which type of flowering plant you have found. The arrows and numbers in the right-hand margin tell you which page to go to next. Identification pages consist of double-page colour plates illustrating some of the individual species in each family. Alongside each illustration are notes on the habitat of the plant, the time of year it can be seen and its size. Measurements are given in millimetres or centimetres – abbreviated to mm or cm (1 cm = 10 mm = 2/5th inch).

The coloured band at the top of each double-page spread helps you locate the relevant parts of the book: *blue* for Introduction, *yellow* for Clues, *red* for Identification. An arrowhead at the top right of a page or spread shows the topic continues on to the next page or spread. A bar at the top right indicates the end of that topic.

Most of us find flowers very attractive and sweet to smell. But for the plant, the flowers are important because they contain the male and female reproductive parts. The male parts of the flower – the **ANTHERS** – produce pollen. Pollen fertilises the female parts – the **OVULES** – in the ovary. In some species or types of plant, there are separate male flowers (containing only pollen) and female flowers (containing only ovules). However, most species produce flowers with both male and female parts.

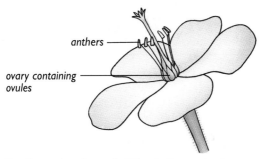

anthers

ovary containing ovules

Once the flower has been fertilised, the ovules become seeds, and the flower changes to become a **FRUIT**. The ovary of the flower becomes the fruit containing the seeds. The job of the fruit is to scatter the new seeds. From each of these seeds, a new plant grows.

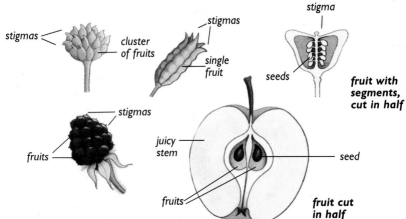

stigmas

cluster of fruits

stigmas

single fruit

stigma

seeds

fruit with segments, cut in half

stigmas

fruits

juicy stem

fruits

seed

fruit cut in half

Flowers have many different shapes and colours. Botanists study the shapes and arrangements of flowers and leaves, and put flowers that are alike into groups called **FAMILIES.** Each family has its own particular shape and arrangement of flower parts.

Most flowers have **PETALS,** usually coloured. Outside these are the green **SEPALS.** In a few species, the petals and sepals are similar in colour, and together form a structure called the **PERIANTH.**

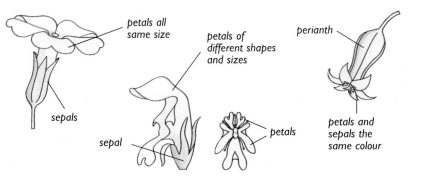

Inside the flower, and next to the petals, sometimes joined to them, are the **STAMENS,** which support the anthers. In the middle of the flower is the **PISTIL,** which receives the pollen. The pistil has a sticky or feathery end called the **STIGMA,** to which the pollen sticks.

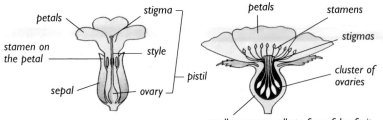

swollen stem swells to form false fruit enclosing cluster of real fruits and seeds

Some flowers have **COMPOSITE** heads. These look like other flowers, but if you look at the 'petals' carefully, you will see that each one is a complete small flower or **FLORET**. The petal-like florets are called strap florets. Some flowers also have cup florets, which form the centre of the flower.

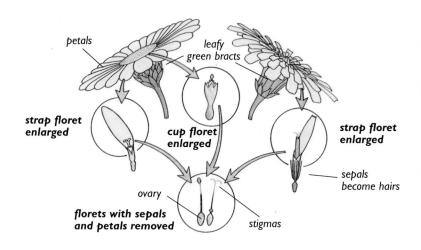

petals

leafy green bracts

strap floret enlarged

cup floret enlarged

strap floret enlarged

sepals become hairs

ovary

florets with sepals and petals removed

stigmas

Flowers may be arranged on stems in many different ways. They may grow singly, or be arranged in groups. Some examples are shown below and on page 7.

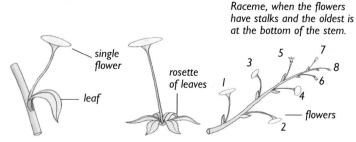

Raceme, when the flowers have stalks and the oldest is at the bottom of the stem.

single flower

leaf

rosette of leaves

flowers

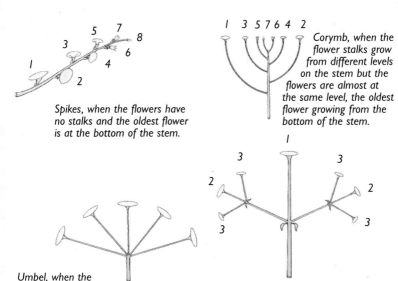

Spikes, when the flowers have no stalks and the oldest flower is at the bottom of the stem.

Corymb, when the flower stalks grow from different levels on the stem but the flowers are almost at the same level, the oldest flower growing from the bottom of the stem.

Umbel, when the flower stalks grow from the same point on the stem.

Cyme, may be two-sided when the flowers grow out from both sides of the stem.

A plant's leaves can give important clues as to what type of plant it is. The leaves may be **SIMPLE**, because they have only one part, or **COMPOUND**, because they have several parts called leaflets.

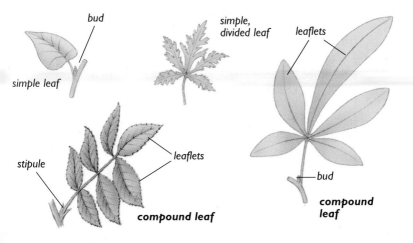

bud

simple leaf

simple, divided leaf

leaflets

stipule

leaflets

compound leaf

bud

compound leaf

CLUE A | If the plant has woody stems it is a tree or shrub. 7

If the stems are *not* woody, go to **CLUE B.**

CLUE B | If the flower has both petals and sepals, go to **CLUE C.**

If each petal-like part is a complete flower called a floret, it is a composite flower (see page 6). 4

If the petals and sepals form a perianth (see page 5) 4

If the flower has no petals or sepals and the perianth is either very small or absent 6

CLUE C | If the flower has petals of different shapes and sizes 3

If the flower has petals of the same shape and size, go to **CLUE D.**

CLUE D | If the petals are joined together 2

petals joined

If the petals are *not* joined together, go to **CLUE E.**

one petal

CLUE E | If the flower has 4 petals, go to **CLUE F.**

If the flower has 5 petals (sometimes more), go to **CLUE G**.

Regular flowers with free petals

CLUE F

If the flower has 6 stamens, 4 long and 2 short, and the ovary is inside the petals it belongs to the **WALLFLOWER FAMILY.**

 12

If the flower has 4 stamens and the ovary is below the petals it belongs to the **WILLOWHERB FAMILY.**

 14

If the flower has many stamens and the stem has a milky or coloured juice it belongs to the **POPPY FAMILY.**

 14

If the flower has many stamens and the stem does *not* have a milky or coloured juice it may be **TORMENTIL** (Rose family).

 21

CLUE G

If the flower has many stamens joined together and leaves in opposite pairs it belongs to the **ST. JOHN'S WORT FAMILY**

leaves in opposite pairs

 16

If the flower has many stamens joined together and leaves in a spiral it belongs to the **MALLOW FAMILY.**

 17

If the flower has 5 stamens or 10 stamens

 11

If the flower has more than 10 separate stamens, go to **CLUE H** overleaf.

CLUE H

If the flower has one or more ovaries below the petals, often inside a swollen stem, and leaves with stipules, it belongs to the **ROSE FAMILY**.

juicy false fruits

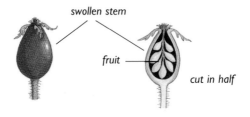

swollen stem

fruit

cut in half

If the flower has one or more ovaries *not* below the petals, and the leaves have leaflets and stipules (see page 7), it belongs to the **ROSE FAMILY**.

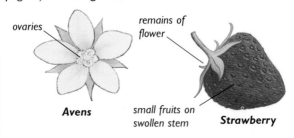

ovaries

remains of flower

Avens

small fruits on swollen stem

Strawberry

If the flower has clusters of ovaries above the petals, and the leaves do *not* have stipules, it belongs to the **BUTTERCUP FAMILY**.

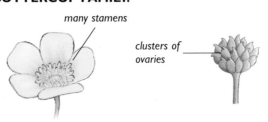

many stamens

clusters of ovaries

CLUE I

If the flowers are arranged in a two-sided cyme (see page 7) it belongs in the **PINK FAMILY.**

24

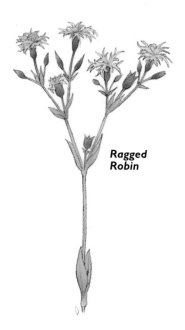

Ragged Robin

If the flowers are solitary, or a few together, and the fruit separates into parts like this, it belongs to the **GERANIUM FAMILY.**

26

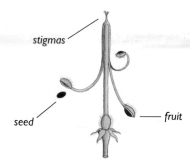

stigmas

seed

fruit

WALLFLOWER FAMILY Cruciferae

If the fruits are much longer than they are wide, it may be

Wallflower
cliffs
April–June 20–60 cm.

Watercress
shallow water
April–Oct 10–60 cm.

Cuckoo Flower
damp meadows
April–June 30–60 cm.

Field Cabbage
fields, waste places
May–Aug 30–60 cm.

Garlic Mustard
(smells of onion) hedges
April–June 20–120 cm.

Hedge Mustard
roadsides, waste places
June–July 30–90 cm.

Charlock
fields, waste places
June–Aug 30–80 cm.

If the fruits are about as wide as they are long, it may be

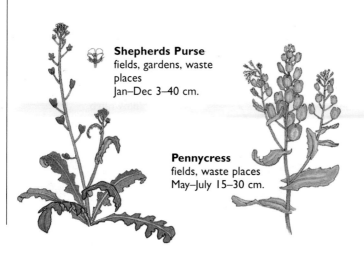

Shepherds Purse
fields, gardens, waste places
Jan–Dec 3–40 cm.

Pennycress
fields, waste places
May–July 15–30 cm.

POPPY FAMILY
Papaveraceae

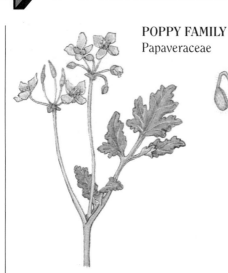

Greater Celandine
hedgerows, waste places
May–Aug 30–90 cm.

Field Poppy
fields, waste places
July–Sept 20–60 cm.

WILLOWHERB
FAMILY
Onagraceae

**Enchanter's
Nightshade**
woods
June–Aug
30–60 cm.

Great Willowherb
ditches, wet places
July–Aug 80–150 cm.

WILLOWHERB FAMILY *continued*

Rosebay Willowherb
banks, waste places
July–Sept 30–120 cm

Pale Willowherb
damp woods, copses
July–Aug 25–60 cm.

Broadleaved Willowherb
hedgerows, woods
June–Aug 20–60 cm.

LOOSESTRIFE FAMILY Lythraceae

If the flowers are not quite like the Willowherbs, it may be

Purple Loosestrife
wet ditches, marshy places
June–Aug 60–120 cm.

ST. JOHN'S WORT FAMILY Hypericaceae

Common St. John's Wort
woods, hedgerows
June–Sept 30–90 cm.

Slender St. John's Wort
dry woods, open heaths
June–Aug 30–60 cm.

WATERLILY FAMILY Nymphaceae

Flowers have many petals and stamens, and leaves float on water

Yellow Waterlily
lakes, slow rivers
July–Aug leaf 12 x 9–40 x 30 cm.

White Waterlily
lakes, slow rivers
July–Aug leaf 10–30 cm.
almost circular

MALLOW FAMILY Malvaceae

Mallow
hedgerows, waste places
June–Sept 45–90 cm.

**Cut-leaved or
Musk Mallow**
hedgerows
July–Aug 30–80 cm.

ROSE FAMILY Rosaceae

If the flowers grow on a tree or bush, they may be

**Blackthorn
(Sloe)**
hedges
March–May
100–400 cm.

Hawthorn (May)
woods, hedges
May–June
200–500 cm.

Crab Apple
woods, hedges
May
200–600 cm.

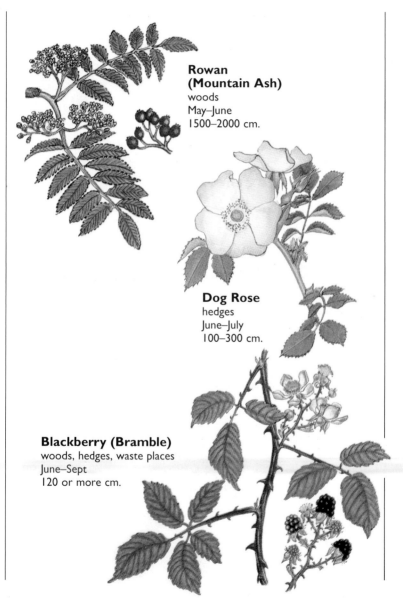

**Rowan
(Mountain Ash)**
woods
May–June
1500–2000 cm.

Dog Rose
hedges
June–July
100–300 cm.

Blackberry (Bramble)
woods, hedges, waste places
June–Sept
120 or more cm.

ROSE FAMILY *continued*

If the plant is not woody, it may be

Wild Strawberry
woods, grassland
April–July
5–30 cm.

Cinquefoil
meadows, hedgerows
June–Sept
30 and more cm.

Silverweed
roadsides, waste
places
June–Aug
24 and more cm.

Tormentil
heaths, dry grassland
June–Sept
5–30 cm.

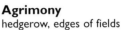

Agrimony
hedgerow, edges of fields
June–Aug
30–60 cm.

Avens
hedgerows, roadsides
June–Aug 20–60 cm.

Meadowsweet
wet places, ditches
June–Sept
60–120 cm.

BUTTERCUP FAMILY Ranunculaceae

Lesser Celandine
fields, waste places
Mar–May
5–25 cm.

Bulbous Buttercup
meadows, waste places
May–June 15–40 cm.

Water Crowfoot
ponds, streams
June–Aug 15–100 cm.

Field Buttercup
meadows,
waste
places
June–Aug
15–100 cm.

**Lesser
Spearwort**
marshes
June–Sept
8–50 cm

Creeping Buttercup
fields, gardens, waste places
May–Aug 15–60 cm.

**Clematis
(Old Man's Beard)**
woody climber with
clusters of whitish, feathery
fruits, hedges, woods
July–Sept 180 and more cm.

If the flower has coloured sepals
and no real petals, it may be

Wood Anemone
woods
March–May
6–30 cm.

Marsh Marigold
marshes
March–July
30–45 cm.

PINK FAMILY Caryophyllaceae

If the sepals are joined together, it may be

Bladder Campion
fields, waste places,
often near the sea
(Sea Campion)
June–Aug 25–90 cm.

White Campion
hedges, fields, waste places
May–Sept 30–100 cm.

Ragged Robin
wet meadows, ditches
May–June 15–75 cm.

Red Campion
woods, hedgerows
May–June 20–90 cm.

If the sepals are not joined
together, it may be

Greater Stitchwort
hedgerows, woods
May–June 15–60 cm.

Mouse-eared Chickweed
woods, fields, waste places
April–Sept 15–45 cm.

If the sepals are not joined together and the plant is trailing,
it may be

Chickweed
fields, gardens, waste places
Jan–Dec 5–40 cm.

Pearlwort
waste and stony places
April–Aug 3–18 cm.

GERANIUM FAMILY Geraniaceae

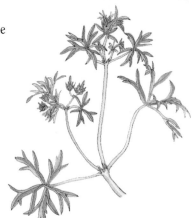

Cut-leaved Cranesbill
dry pastures, waste places
April–Aug 10–60 cm.

Dovesfoot Cranesbill
waste and cultivated places
April–Sept 10–40 cm.

Meadow Cranesbill
meadows, hedgerows
June–Sept 30–80 cm.

Herb Robert
woods, cultivated places
May–Sept 10–50 cm.

Regular flowers with joined petals

LUE A

If the petal tube separates at the top into 5 parts, go to **CLUE B.**

If the petal tube separates at the top into 4 parts and the plant has leaves in whorls, it belongs to the **BEDSTRAW FAMILY.**

 29

leaves in whorls

CLUE B | If the ovary grows inside the flower, and the stamens are attached to the petals, go to **CLUE C.**

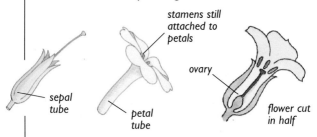

stamens still attached to petals

ovary

sepal tube

petal tube

flower cut in half

If the ovary grows below the petals, and the stamens are *not* attached to the petals, it belongs to the **BELLFLOWER FAMILY.**

stamens

 2

ovary

petals

CLUE C

If the flowers are arranged in a one-sided cyme (see page 7) it belongs to the **BORAGE FAMILY** or **NIGHTSHADE FAMILY.**

 3

If the flowers grow singly, or are arranged in umbels or racemes (see pages 6 and 7) it belongs to the **PRIMROSE FAMILY.**

 3

BEDSTRAW FAMILY
Rubiaceae

Goosegrass
hedgerows
June–Aug
15–120 cm.

Hedge Bedstraw
hedgerows
June–July
25–120 cm.

Heath Bedstraw
open heaths
July–Aug
10–20 cm.

Ladies' Bedstraw
banks,
grassland
July–Aug
15–100 cm

BELLFLOWER FAMILY Campanulaceae

Harebell
hilly grasslands
July–Sept
15–40 cm.

Nettle-leaved Bellflower
hedgebanks, woods
July–Aug
50–100 cm.

BORAGE FAMILY Boraginaceae

Comfrey
moist banks,
meadows
May–Aug
30–120 cm.

Water Forget-me-not
shiny leaves, wet
ditches
June–Aug 15–45 cm.

Field Forget-me-not
hedge banks
June–Sept 15–30 cm.

NIGHTSHADE FAMILY
Solanaceae

Deadly Nightshade
waste stony places, chalk
or limestone soils
June–Aug
100–150 cm.

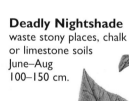

Woody Nightshade (Bittersweet)
hedges
30–200 cm.

Black Nightshade
fields, gardens
June–Sept 30–60 cm.

PRIMROSE FAMILY Primulaceae

Yellow Pimpernel
woods, shady hedgerows
May–Sept
15–40 cm.

Primrose
woods, banks
Dec–May
8–15 cm.

Cowslip
meadows, grassy slopes
April–May
5–15 cm.

Scarlet Pimpernel
weed in cultivated land,
waste places
June–Aug 6–30 cm.

Yellow Loosestrife
shady banks, near
streams, gardens
May–Sept 60–150 cm.

Creeping Jenny
wet banks, gardens
June–Aug 30–60 cm.

32 CLUES TO FLOWERS – 3

Irregular flowers

CLUE A

If the petals are flat and only slightly different in shape, go to **CLUE B**.

If the petals are very different in shape and size, go to **CLUE D**.

CLUE B

If the flowers are arranged in umbels of umbels (see page 7), it belongs to the **PARSLEY FAMILY**.

3

If the flowers are *not* arranged in this way, go to **CLUE C**.

CLUE C

If the flowers have 4 petals joined together, only 2 stamens and a double ovary they are **SPEEDWELLS** and belong to the Foxglove family.

3

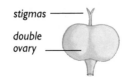

stigmas

double ovary

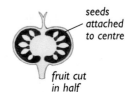

seeds attached to centre

fruit cut in half

CLUE C
continued

If the flowers have 5 petals, 5 stamens, and the ovary has 3 parts with seeds attached to each part, it belongs to the **VIOLET FAMILY.**

 40

seeds — ovary cut across

seeds — fruit after opening

CLUE D

If the petals are joined together, go to **CLUE E.**

If the petals are *not* joined together and are arranged as below, if the stalks of the stamens are joined together, and the fruit is a pod, it belongs to the **PEA FAMILY.**

 40

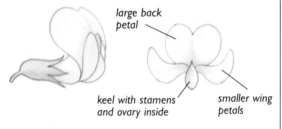

large back petal

keel with stamens and ovary inside

smaller wing petals

CLUE E

If the plant has square stems, leaves arranged in opposite pairs, flowers with 4 stamens, and the fruit looks like a hot-cross bun, it belongs to the **DEADNETTLE FAMILY.**

 44

If the plant has square stems, but the fruit is *not* like a hot-cross bun, it may be a **FIGWORT** and belongs to the Foxglove family.

39

If the plant does *not* have square stems and the fruits are double (see page 32), it belongs to the **FOXGLOVE FAMILY.**

 38

PARSLEY FAMILY Umbelliferae

If the fruits are smooth, it may be

Chervil (Cow Parsley)
hedgerows
March–May
30–50 cm.

Earthnut
woods, meadows
May–June
30–50 cm.

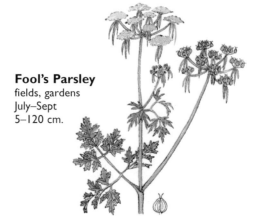

Fool's Parsley
fields, gardens
July–Sept
5–120 cm.

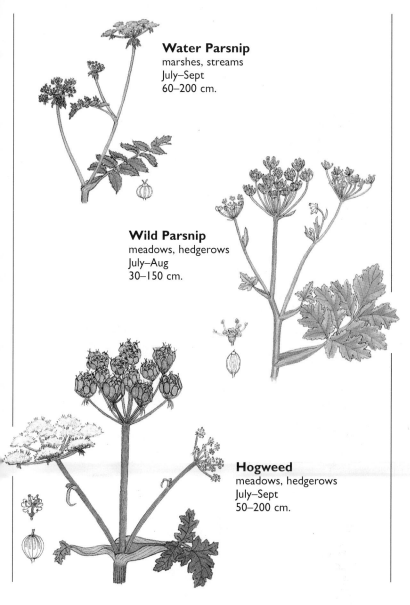

Water Parsnip
marshes, streams
July–Sept
60–200 cm.

Wild Parsnip
meadows, hedgerows
July–Aug
30–150 cm.

Hogweed
meadows, hedgerows
July–Sept
50–200 cm.

PARSLEY FAMILY *continued*

If the fruits are smooth, it may be

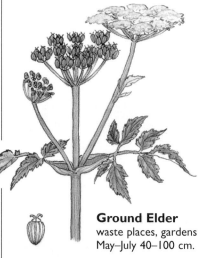

Ground Elder
waste places, gardens
May–July 40–100 cm.

If the fruits are prickly, it may be

Rough Chervil
hedgerows, grassy places
June–July
30–100 cm.

Wild Carrot
fields, waste places
June–Sept
30–100 cm.

If the fruits are
prickly, it may be

Hedge Parsley
hedgerows, waste places
July–Sept
5–125 cm.

FOXGLOVE FAMILY Scrophulariaceae

If the flowers are almost flat, it may be

**Germander
Speedwell**
woods, grassland,
hedgerows
May–Aug 20–40 cm.

**Common
Speedwell**
woods, dry grassland
June–Aug
10–40 cm.

Brooklime
wet ditches,
streams
June–Aug
20–60 cm.

FOXGLOVE FAMILY *continued*

If flowers are almost flat, it may be

Great Mullein
roadsides, waste places
July–Aug
20–300 cm.

Thyme-leaved Speedwell
fields, waste places
June–Aug
10–30 cm.

Buxbaum's Speedwell
cultivated fields, gardens
Jan–Dec
10–40 cm.

If the petals are very different and are joined to make a tube, it may be

Foxglove
dry banks, roadsides
June–Aug
50–150 cm.

Yellow Rattle
dry pastures
May–June
20–50 cm.

Eyebright
grassland
June–Sept
5–30 cm.

If the petals are very different and are joined to make a tube, it may be

Figwort
wet meadows, waste places
June–Aug
40–80 cm.

Lousewort
damp grassland
June–Aug
8–25 cm.

If the petals have a spur at the base, it may be

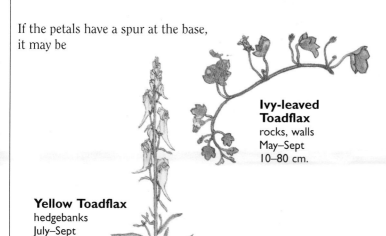

Ivy-leaved Toadflax
rocks, walls
May–Sept
10–80 cm.

Yellow Toadflax
hedgebanks
July–Sept
30–80 cm.

VIOLET FAMILY Violaceae

Dog Violet
woods, banks, heaths
April–June 2–20 cm.

Heartsease
cultivated and waste ground
April–Sept 3–45 cm.

Sweet Violet
banks, woods
Feb–April 6–12 cm.

PEA FAMILY Leguminosae

If the plant has leaves with three leaflets, it may be

Spotted Medick
waste places
April–Aug
10–60 cm.

Black Medick
waste places, grassland
April–Aug
5–50 cm.

If the plant has leaves with three
leaflets, it may be

Hop Trefoil
dry meadows
June–Sept 30–35 cm.

Bird's foot Trefoil
meadows, grassland
June–Sept
10–40 cm.

White Clover
meadows, grassland
June–Sept
30–50 cm.

Red Clover
meadows, grassland
May–Sept
30–60 cm.

Broom
(woody stems)
heaths, waste places
May–June
60–200 cm.

PEA FAMILY *continued*

If the plant has many leaflets and some tendrils, it may be a Vetch.

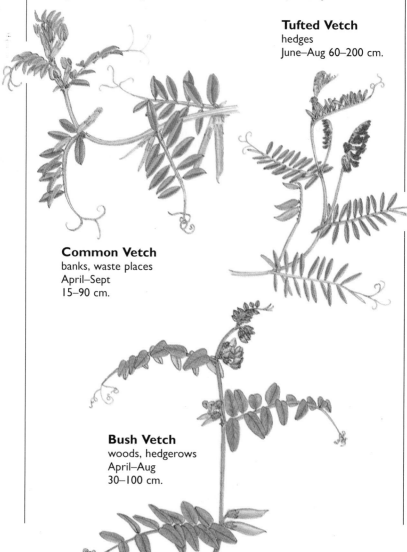

Tufted Vetch
hedges
June–Aug 60–200 cm.

Common Vetch
banks, waste places
April–Sept
15–90 cm.

Bush Vetch
woods, hedgerows
April–Aug
30–100 cm.

If the plant has only 2 or 3 pairs of leaflets and tendrils, it may be

Meadow Pea
moist meadows
April–Aug
30–120 cm.

If the plant has prickles it is

Gorse
(woody stems)
sandy heaths
March–June
60–200 cm.

DEADNETTLE FAMILY Labiatae

If the top petals form a hood and the leaves are strongly scented when squeezed, it may be

Thyme
heaths, dry grassland
June–Aug
5–7 cm.

Marjoram
hilly grasslands, woods
July–Sept
30–80 cm.

Woundwort
ditches, shady banks
July–Aug
30–100 cm.

If the leaves are faintly scented it may be

Wild Basil
roadsides, wood edges,
leaves downy
July–Sept
10–40 cm.

Ground Ivy
hedges, woods,
waste places
March–May
10–30 cm.

If the petals are almost the same size, it may be

Water Mint
wet ditches, marshes
July–Oct
15–90 cm.

Corn Mint
woods, wet ground,
cultivated fields
Aug–Oct
10–60 cm.

DEADNETTLE FAMILY *continued*

If the top petals form a hood and
the leaves are **not** strongly scented,
it may be

Red Deadnettle
garden weed, waste places
March–Oct
10–45 cm.

Wood Sage
dry, heathy places
July–Sept
20–30 cm.

Self-heal
banks, grassland
June–Sept
5–30 cm.

Betony
open woods, hedgebanks,
grassland, heaths
June–Sept 15–60 cm.

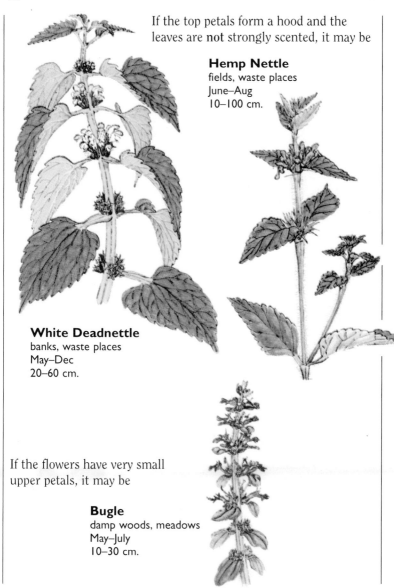

If the top petals form a hood and the leaves are **not** strongly scented, it may be

Hemp Nettle
fields, waste places
June–Aug
10–100 cm.

White Deadnettle
banks, waste places
May–Dec
20–60 cm.

If the flowers have very small upper petals, it may be

Bugle
damp woods, meadows
May–July
10–30 cm.

48 CLUES TO FLOWERS – 4

CLUE A | If each floret has 4 separate stamens and a single stigma it belongs to the **SCABIOUS FAMILY.**

 5

If each floret has 5 stamens joined at the top and a stigma that divides into 2 parts it belongs to the **DAISY FAMILY.**

5

CLUE B | If the perianth is small, green or brown or pinkish, go to **CLUE C.**

If the perianth is large and petal-like

6

CLUE C | If the leaves have net veins, go to **CLUE D.**

If the leaves have parallel veins it belongs to the **RUSH FAMILY.**

 5

CLUE D | If the leaves grow in a rosette, and the flower stalk has no leaves, it belongs to the **PLANTAIN FAMILY.**

 5

CLUE D
continued

If the stems are leafy, with many clusters of flowers, usually in spikes and racemes (see page 7), go to **CLUE E**.

CLUE E

If the flower look likes this it belongs to the **SPURGE FAMILY**.

59

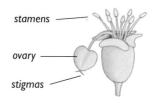

stamens

ovary

stigmas

If the flowers have either stamens or ovary, but *not* both, it may be **DOG'S MERCURY** (Spurge Family).

59

If the flowers are *not* like this, go to **CLUE F**.

CLUE F

If the leaves have stipules forming a sheath round the stem it belongs to the **DOCK FAMILY**.

60

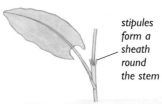

stipules form a sheath round the stem

If the leaves do *not* have stipules, go to **CLUE G**.

CLUE G

If the leaves have stinging hairs, it belongs to the **NETTLE FAMILY**.

If the leaves do *not* have stinging hairs, it belongs to the **GOOSEFOOT FAMILY**.

61
61

SCABIOUS FAMILY Dipsacaceae

Field Scabious
woods, grasslands,
hedgerows
July–Sept
25–100 cm.

Teasel
roadsides, waste places
July–Aug
50–200 cm.

DAISY FAMILY Compositae

If the florets are cup-shaped in the centre, strap-shaped round the outside and have no pappus (a 'parachute' of fine hairs on the seed) it may be

Moon Daisy
grasslands
June–Aug
20–70 cm.

Feverfew
(strongly scented)
walls and waste places
July–Aug
25–60 cm.

If the florets are cup-shaped in the centre, strap-shaped round the outside and have no pappus it may be

Daisy
short grassland
March–Oct
2–4 cm.

Yarrow
meadows, hedgebanks
June–Aug
8–45 cm.

No cup-shaped
florets

Stinking Mayweed
(strongly scented)
fields, waste places
July–Sept
20–60 cm.

**Scentless
Mayweed**
fields, waste places
July–Sept
10–60 cm.

Pineapple Weed
(strongly scented)
roadsides, waste places
June–July 5–30 cm.

DAISY FAMILY *continued*

If all the florets are strap-shaped and yellow, and the pappus is feathery, it may be

Goat's-beard
meadows
June–July
30–70 cm.

Cat's Ear
(no scales between
the florets)
meadows, waste
places
June–Sept
30–60 cm.

Autumnal
Hawkbit
(scales between
the florets)
meadows
June–Sept
5–60 cm.

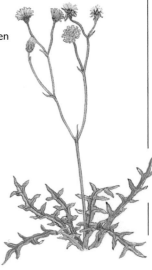

Common
Hawkbit
(scales between
the florets)
meadows
June–Sept
15–30 cm.

If all the florets are strap-shaped and there is no pappus it may be

Nipplewort
waste places, gardens
July–Sept 20–90 cm.

If all the florets are cup-shaped in the centre and strap-shaped round the outside and there is a pappus it may be

Golden Rod
woods
June–Sept
5–75 cm.

Ragwort
roadside, waste places
July–Sept
30–150 cm

DAISY FAMILY *continued*

If all the florets are strap-shaped and yellow, and the pappus has simple hairs, it may be

Dandelion
meadows, waste places
March–Oct
5–20 cm.

Smooth Hawk's-beard
dry banks, waste places
June–Sept
20–90 cm.

Common Hawkweed
banks, woods, meadows
July–Aug
20–80 cm.

If all the florets are strap-shaped
and yellow, and the pappus has
simple hairs, it may be

Sow Thistle
(stem has a milky juice)
fields, waste places
June–Aug
20–150 cm.

If the florets are all cup-
shaped but the fruit has
no pappus it may be

Mugwort
(strongly scented)
waste places
July–Sept
60–120 cm.

Tansy
(strongly scented)
edges of fields, roadsides,
waste places
July–Sept 30–100 cm.

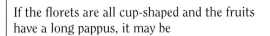

DAISY FAMILY *continued*

If the florets are all cup-shaped and the fruits
have a long pappus, it may be

Creeping Thistle
fields, waste places
July–Sept
30–90 cm.

Spear Thistle
fields, waste places
July–Oct
30–150 cm.

Coltsfoot
(flowers appear
before the leaves)
roadsides, waste places
Feb–April. 5–15 cm.

Groundsel
fields, gardens
Jan–Dec
8–45 cm.

If the florets are all cup-shaped and the fruits have a short, stiff pappus, it may be

Lesser Knapweed
or Hardhead
meadows, roadsides
June–Sept
15–60 cm.

Greater Knapweed
dry meadows,
roadsides
July–Sept
30–90 cm.

Burdock
roadsides, waste places
June–Aug
60–120 cm.

RUSH FAMILY Juncaceae

If the plant has long round leaves it may be

Common Rush
wet places
June–Aug
30–150 cm.

Hard Rush
wet places
June–Aug
25–60 cm.

Toad Rush
wet places
May–Sept
3–25 cm.

Jointed Rush
(ridges can be felt in the leaves)
wet places
June–Sept
25–80 cm.

If the plant has flat,
hairy leaves it may be

Woodrush
woods, dry places
March–June
15–30 cm.

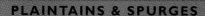
PLANTAIN FAMILY Plantaginaceae

Ribwort
waste places,
grassland
April–Aug
10–15 cm.

Greater Plantain
roadsides, grass,
cultivated land
May–Sept
10–15 cm.

SPURGE FAMILY Euphorbiaceae

Dog's Mercury
woods
Feb–March
15–40 cm.

Petty Spurge
cultivated and waste
ground
April–Nov
10–30 cm.

Sun Spurge
cultivated ground
May–Oct
10–50 cm.

DOCK FAMILY Polygonaceae

Flowers with 6 perianth parts

Curled Dock or Broad-leaved Dock
grassy places, waste ground, shingle beaches
June–Oct
50–100 cm.

fruit of Curled Dock

fruit of Broad-leaved Dock

Sorrel
wet meadows
May–June
30–100 cm.

Sheep's Sorrel
dry meadows
May–Aug 10–30 cm.

Flowers with 5 perianth parts

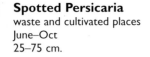

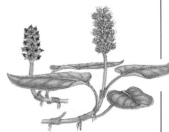

Spotted Persicaria
waste and cultivated places
June–Oct
25–75 cm.

Amphibious Persicaria
in ponds the leaves float
July–Sept
30–75 cm.

Knotgrass
cultivated and waste places
July–Oct
10–40 cm.

GOOSEFOOT FAMILY Chenopodiaceae

Stamens and ovaries
in the same flower

Wild Beet
seashore
July–Sept
30–120 cm.

White Goosefoot
leaves powdery,
gardens, waste places
July–Oct
30–60 cm.

Stamens and
ovaries in
separate flowers

Common Orache
leaves powdery,
gardens, waste places
Aug–Oct. 30–90 cm.

NETTLE FAMILY Urticaceae

Stinging Nettle
banks, woods, near farms
June–Aug
30–150 cm.

62 CLUES TO FLOWERS – 5

6

Flowers with a large perianth

CLUE A If the perianth parts are very different in shape and size it belongs to the **ORCHID FAMILY.**

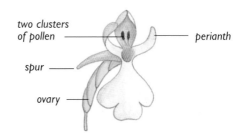

two clusters of pollen — — perianth

spur —

ovary —

If the perianth is *not* like this, go to **CLUE B.**

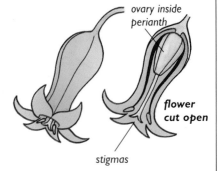

ovary inside perianth

flower cut open

stigmas

CLUE B If the ovary is inside the perianth, go to **CLUE C.**

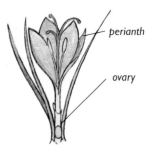

perianth

ovary

If the ovary is below the perianth, go to **CLUE D.**

CLUE C

If the ovary is a cluster of separate parts, and the leaves have net veins, it belongs to the **BUTTERCUP FAMILY.**

 23

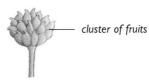

cluster of fruits

If the ovary is a cluster of separate parts, and the leaves have parallel veins, it belongs to the **WATER PLANTAIN FAMILY.**

 65

If the ovary is single with 3 divisions, it belongs to the **LILY FAMILY.**

 66

ovary cut across

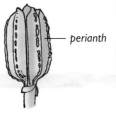

perianth

CLUE D

If the flower has 3 stamens it belongs to the **IRIS FAMILY.**

66

If the flower has 6 stamens, it belongs to the **SNOWDROP FAMILY.**

 67

ORCHID FAMILY Orchidaceae

If the flower has a short spur it may be

Early Purple Orchid
woods, grasslands
April–June
15–60 cm.

Spotted Orchid
marshes, damp meadows
June–Aug
15–60 cm.

If the flower has large lower
petals that look like an
insect's body it may be

Bee Orchid
chalk and limestone banks
June–July
15–45 cm.

If the flower has a long, slender spur it may be

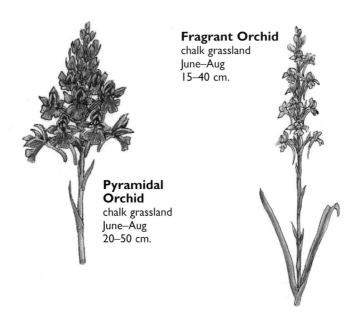

Fragrant Orchid
chalk grassland
June–Aug
15–40 cm.

**Pyramidal
Orchid**
chalk grassland
June–Aug
20–50 cm.

WATER PLANTAIN FAMILY
Alismataceae

Water Plantain
watery ditches, edges of streams
June–Aug
20–100 cm.

LILY FAMILY Liliaceae

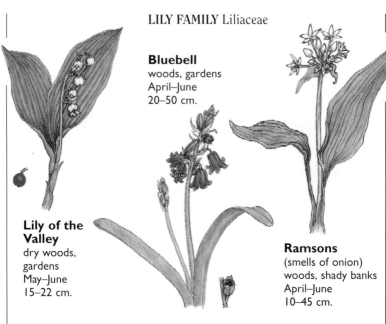

Bluebell
woods, gardens
April–June
20–50 cm.

Lily of the Valley
dry woods,
gardens
May–June
15–22 cm.

Ramsons
(smells of onion)
woods, shady banks
April–June
10–45 cm.

IRIS FAMILY Iridaceae

Crocus
garden escapes, meadows
March–April
10–15 cm.

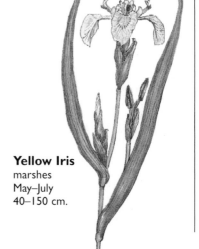

Yellow Iris
marshes
May–July
40–150 cm.

FLAX FAMILY
Linaceae

CONVOLVULUS FAMILY
Convolvulaceae

Convolvulus (Lesser Bindweed)
fields, pastures
May–Sept
20–75 cm.

Fairy Flax
meadows, pastures
June–Aug
5–25 cm.

SNOWDROP FAMILY Amaryllidaceae

Snowdrop
damp woods, gardens
Jan–March
15–25 cm.

Daffodil
damp woods, grassland, gardens
March–April
20–35 cm.

Flowers with no petals or sepals, perianth small or absent

CLUE A

If the plant has leaves that float on or grow under the water it belongs to the **PONDWEED FAMILY**.

7

If the plant does *not* grow in water and has grass-like leaves with parallel veins, go to **CLUE B**.

CLUE B

If the stem is hollow and there is a leafy ligule where the leaf sheath begins and stamens and pistil in the same flower, it belongs to the **GRASS FAMILY**.

6

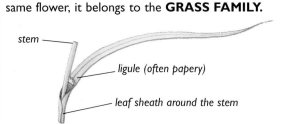

stem —

—— ligule (often papery)

—— leaf sheath around the stem

If the stem is solid and often 3-sided, with no ligule where the sheath begins and has separate flowers, it belongs to the **SEDGE FAMILY**.

7

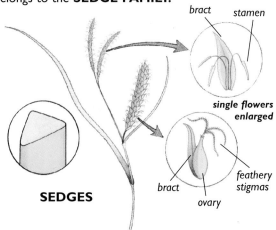

bract   stamen

single flowers enlarged

feathery stigmas

SEDGES

bract

ovary

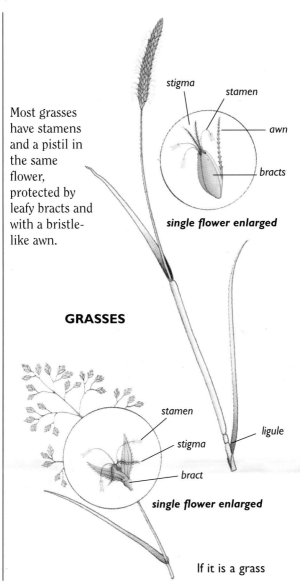

Most grasses have stamens and a pistil in the same flower, protected by leafy bracts and with a bristle-like awn.

stigma *stamen* *awn* *bracts*

single flower enlarged

GRASSES

stamen *stigma* *bract* *ligule*

single flower enlarged

If it is a grass

 70

 70

GRASS FAMILY Gramineae

If the flowers are arranged in tight spikes it may be

Sweet Vernal
(scented)
meadows
May–July
20–50 cm.

Timothy
(no scent, spiky)
meadows
July
50–100 cm.

or
Cat's Tail
(flower spike)
meadows
50 cm or less.

Fox Tail
(soft) damp
grassland
April–June
30–90 cm.

awns

Meadow Barley
meadows
June–July
30–60 cm.

If the flowers are
in stalkless
clusters it may be

Couch Grass
fields, waste places
June–Sept
30–100 cm.

Rye Grass
waste places,
grassland
May–Aug
25–50 cm.

If the flowers are in stalked
clusters it may be

Cock's Foot Grass
meadows, roadsides
May–July
30–100 cm.

GRASS FAMILY *continued*

If the flowers have awns and are in spreading clusters it may be

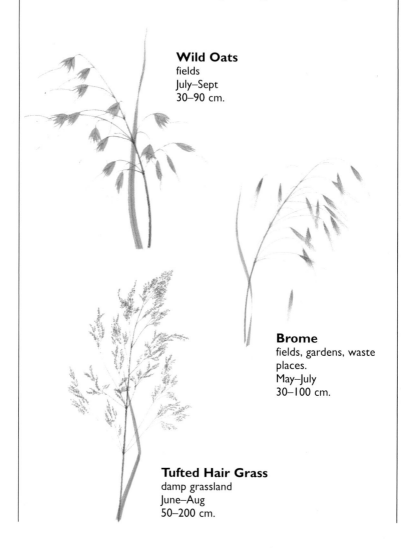

Wild Oats
fields
July–Sept
30–90 cm.

Brome
fields, gardens, waste
places.
May–July
30–100 cm.

Tufted Hair Grass
damp grassland
June–Aug
50–200 cm.

If the flowers do not have awns and are in spreading clusters it may be

Bent
grasslands
June–Aug
20–50 cm.

Soft Grass
meadows
July–July
20–60 cm.

Quaking Grass
hill slopes
June–July
20–50 cm.

Meadow Grass
meadows
May–July
15–80 cm.

Great Water Grass
edges of lakes and rivers
July–Aug. 60–70 cm.
not to confused with **Reed Grass**
(Phragmites) which has awns

SEDGE FAMILY Cyperaceae

If the stamens and ovaries are in separate flowers in the same cluster it may be

Common Bulrush
lakes, ponds, wet ditches
June–Aug
100–300 cm.

If the stamens and ovaries are in separate clusters of flowers it may be

Carnation Sedge
damp places
May–June
10–40 cm.

Common Sedge
marshes, wet grassland
May–Aug
7–70 cm.

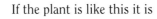

If the plant is like this it is

Reedmace *(Typhaceae)*
(sometimes wrongly called
bulrush)
lakes, ponds wet ditches
June–Aug 150–250 cm.

PONDWEED FAMILY Potamogetonaceae

All pondweeds grow in water and have very long stems

Broad-leaved Pondweed
lakes, ponds, streams
May–Sept

Opposite-leaved Pondweed
shallow pools, ditches
May–Sept

Curled Pondweed
lakes, ponds, streams
May–Oct

Canadian Pondweed
(Hydrocharidaceae)
lakes, ponds,
streams
May–Oct

DUCKWEED FAMILY Lemnaceae

These plants float freely on water; flowers not often seen

Lesser Duckweed
ponds
June–July
1.5–4 mm across

Ivy Leaved Duckweed
ponds
May–July
7–12 mm across

Flowers of plants with woody stems
Only one or two tree types are identified here. Look
in a book on trees and shrubs to find out more.

CLUE A If the fruit is a cone and the leaves are small and
needle-like it belongs to the **CONIFERS.**

If the fruit is *not* a
cone and the leaves
are net-veined, go
to **CLUE B.**

CLUE B If the flowers with
stamens are arranged
in catkins

Hazel catkins

CLUE B continued

Many trees have two kinds of flower: clusters of flowers with stamens forming catkins, and flowers with a pistil that are less easy to see.

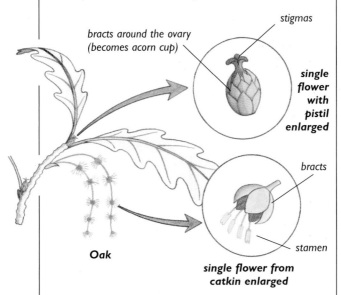

bracts around the ovary (becomes acorn cup)

stigmas

single flower with pistil enlarged

bracts

stamen

Oak

single flower from catkin enlarged

If the flowers are *not* arranged in catkins, go to **CLUE C**.

CLUE C

If the flowers are like those of the **PEA FAMILY** 34

If the flowers are like those of the **ROSE FAMILY** 18

If the flowers are like those of the **BUTTERCUP FAMILY**, and the plant climbs, it is **CLEMATIS**. 23

If the flowers are *not* like these 78

HEATHER FAMILY Ericaceae

Bell Heather
dry heaths
July–Sept
60 cm.

Ling
heaths
July–Sept
60 cm.

CONIFERS

Pine
heathlands
May–June

Yew
hilly places
March–April

IVY FAMILY Araliaceae

Ivy
(woody climber with roots in the ground. Not a parasite).
walls, trees
Sept–Nov

BROADLEAVES

Hazel (*Corylaceae*)
woods, hedges
Jan–April

Oak (*Fagaceae*)
woods, hedgerows
April–May

Clues for the basic features of all flower families start on page 8.

Further Reading

Blamey, Marjorie and Christopher Grey-Wilson, *Illustrated Flora of Britain and Northern Europe*. Hodder, 1989.
Burnie, David, *Flowers*. Eyewitness Explorer Series, Dorling Kindersley, 1996.
Edlin, Herbert L., *The Tree Key*. Warne, 1978.
Rose, Francis, *Wild Flower Key: British Isles and Europe*. Warne 1991.
Sutton, David, *Field Guide to Wild Flowers of Britain and Europe*. Kingfisher, 1988.

A good way to learn more about the animals and plants in your area is to join Wildlife Watch, a club for young people interested in wildlife and the environment. As well as organising activities for its members, Watch produces a national magazine, local newsletters, and many posters and activity packs. Their address is Wildlife Watch, The Green, Witham Park, Waterside South, Lincoln LN5 7JR.